Stitched Together

STORIES FOR THE QUILTER'S SOUL

 VOLUME 1

MISSOURI STAR
QUILT CO.

Table of Contents

✳

Here at Missouri Star Quilt Co., we've always assumed we're in the business of quilts, not stories, but back in March 2014 we asked you, our readers, to send us the stories of why you quilt. The plan was to publish the three best stories and move on to the next project. We never intended to publish a book. We just wanted to have a contest for National Quilting Month. We had no idea what we were getting ourselves into!

We didn't get a couple hundred responses like we expected to. Instead, we were flooded with over a thousand, and they didn't stop coming! You told us your stories, opened your hearts and shared your tragedies, triumphs, and laughs. We marveled at your resilience, your generosity, and your quilts! And in the end there was nothing to be done with these treasures but put them in a book so that they could be read and reread and lent to the girls at the quilting circle.

We thought we were in the business of quilts, not stories, but you have taught us that you can't have one without the other. So thank you, and thank you for giving us a glimpse into the many reasons you quilt. You have reminded us why we do too.

Jenny

P.S. We're still getting stories and we're still sharing them. We publish one story every Tuesday on our website at missouriquiltco.com.

The Yellow Quilt

by **MARY SUTHERBY**
Radnor, Pennsylvania

When my elderly Aunt B asked me what I wanted of hers (the Waterford Bowl, the Hummel figurine, collectibles from her world travels), I knew immediately.

"I'd like the yellow quilt."

My mother was born on a farm in Minnesota in 1921 just before the Depression, my Aunt Bernita the year before. Their mother died when they were small. Their father lost everything during the Depression. They took turns working to support each other through nursing school.

My aunt didn't have children of her own so she became the "grandma" we were missing from that side. All of my six brothers and sisters (and their spouses and children) are close to her.

Aunt B moved to Phoenix for a teaching position at Arizona State

University when I was a child. She had a guest room decorated in white and purple with a twin bed and trundle. A handmade yellow quilt covered the bed. I'm sure I slept so well there because of all the mothering she gave me, but over time what I remembered was snoozing under that beautiful old yellow patchwork quilt.

I found my way to San Francisco after college and had the opportunity to be in Phoenix once a month, so I would always forgo the hotel and stay with Aunt B. One evening when she asked me what I would like of hers when she was gone, I surprised her with my request and then she shared the story of the yellow quilt.

Aunt B's best friend's mother made the quilt for her as a graduation gift when she finished nursing school at the U of M in the late 1920s. Even retelling the story six decades later brought tears to her eyes. Aunt B shared that she thought she had probably always missed the nurturing of a mother, since her mother died when she was little. Viv's mother seemed to sense this and had been exceptionally kind and nurturing to her. It was not just that Viv's mother had sewn it especially for Aunt B, it was also that all those little pieces of fabric, old dresses and shirts and pieces from this or that from her life, were stitched together to carry to her own life.

Now Aunt B is 93 and has Alzheimer's, so she lives in a care facility. Recently my brother, his wife, and I sorted through her things to close her home. At one point he said to me "You know, it's time for you to take the yellow quilt." It was all I could do to hold back the tears when I left her condo that day with the yellow quilt under my arm. All the way to the airport, as I looked at it on the plane, and when I spread it out on a bed in my home, I had a lump in my throat.

That was last summer. Last fall, as I was looking at the yellow quilt one day, it got me to thinking about a quilting class I took about ten years ago when my children were young. There just didn't seem to be enough time back then. I got on the computer and starting searching resources on quilting and discovered a whole new world—Precuts, Craftsy, YouTube videos. I got out my old machine and (fighting the tension all the way) made my first mess of a quilt. This led to a new machine and then more online classes and now a guest room taken over with a sewing wall, fabric stash, rotary cutter, and mat. In addition to everything else, that old yellow quilt led me to a new hobby that gives me great peace and joy, and a terrific creative outlet.

The yellow quilt has traveled three generations to the home of a family the quilter would never know. Among all of my aunt's things, to me, it is the most valuable.

Lost But Now Found

by **Sarah Schmachtenberger**
Midvale, Utah

My father was born in 1929 in Oakland, California to a young, single woman. Despite his mother's attempt to raise him as a single parent, she reluctantly surrendered him when he was just one month old to the Children's Aid Society orphanage and he was placed for adoption. Unfortunately, the home that he was placed in didn't allow my father to feel like he fit in or that he belonged. After much persistence, he was able to find out his mother's name, age, and background information. With these details, he searched for her for almost 30 years.

Finally in 2001, after much research and legwork, my step-sister and I were able to locate his mother's family and contact them. We were heartbroken to find out that his mother, my grandmother, had passed away several years after she placed him for adoption. Upon their request, we sent them family photos of myself, my brothers, and my

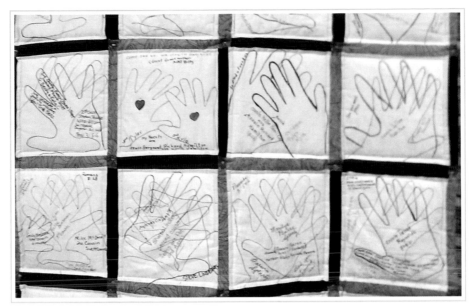

father. They knew instantly we were related, the family resemblance is absolutely incredible.

The family invited my father out to California, hosted a large dinner in his honor, and introduced him to his family. After many hugs and tears, my father met cousins, uncles, and aunts that he never knew he had. After the dinner, they gave him a lovely album of family photos, including those of his mother and grandparents, and a detailed family history.

Then they presented him with the most wonderful gift of all. A quilt that his new aunt had made. At the top it reads "Hands Touching Hands Family Quilt, Together at Last." On each of the blocks each member of our newfound family traced their hands and wrote their names, how

we are related, and a sweet message for my father. He finally felt, after 71 years, like he belonged. On the back of the quilt, they embroidered "Lost but now found. To Jim-Robert Lee Reynolds" (his birth name). My Father cherished this quilt. It meant the world to him. It laid on the foot of his bed while he bravely battled cancer until his death four years ago. It now sits in my home and means so very much to me.

As a quilter myself, I know the power of a quilt. To me, quilting means family, love, and a connection that can span generations, transcend time, and envelop the owner in a hug, a hug especially for them from the dear person or people who made it. When I sit under this quilt I think of my grandmother, my new family, and of my dad.

Beautiful Imperfection

✳

by **ANGELA STANLEY**
Mount Airy, Maryland

My story is as much about a quilt as it is about a little boy. My life was forever changed by the birth of my fourth child. He appeared so healthy, but over the first few weeks of his life it became apparent that there was something wrong. Liver disease we were told... terminal by age two if immediate palliative surgery is not performed... liver transplant is the only cure.

My mind raced as we brought our once perfect son to the hospital. I hadn't quilted or crafted in so many years with my young children underfoot, but as we left I grabbed some sewing supplies. I spent two weeks with my son at the hospital and began creating piles of English paper pieced hexagons in bright rainbow batiks. I cradled my tiny son in my lap and prayed and sewed and prayed some more. My hexagons became flowers by the time he was well enough to go home.

Photos Courtesy Angela Stanley

My son recovered from the surgery on his liver but now had a five-inch scar across his tiny abdomen. Beautiful imperfection, I thought. Just like my quilt.

As my son grew, so did the quilt. His medical needs were very high, even at home, and over the next year he was in the hospital nine additional times for life-threatening infections. Wherever he went, I went, and the quilt went. I held my son and prayed. I watched him sleep in the hospital crib and I sewed and prayed. When my world was spinning out of control and critical information was bombarding me from all directions, I relished the time to sit, be physically and mentally still, and sew. The quilt brought me peace and allowed me to produce something beautiful, bound with threads of fear and anxiety, but also of hope and love.

When my son was fourteen months old, and the quilt was big enough to wrap around his sweetly scarred body, he was finally listed to receive a liver transplant. For two months, both my son and I underwent countless medical tests. I was being evaluated to be a living donor. Much of that two-month period was tense waiting. Would he get another infection? When would a liver come for him? Would I be a match? I think I sewed more on my hexagon flowers in those two months than ever before.

As a full-fledged toddler now, my son knew "his quilt," bright rainbow flowers and all. On July 11, 2013, my son received his new liver. Again, the quilt and I made another journey to the hospital. But this time I was unable to work on it because I too was recovering from surgery. My prayers were answered for my little boy and I was humbled and honored that I was able to give a portion of my liver to my son.

Eight months later, my son and I are fully recovered. The quilt continues to grow and so does my son — truly beautiful imperfection.

Quilting to Contribute

by **Becky Goldner**
Spokane, Washington

Four years ago, I closed my small business to care for my husband who was exhibiting some odd behavior. Turns out the ol' guy has Alzheimer's and every day is a new day. Quilting has become my sanity. It allows me to be at home and yet still contribute to the welfare (be it mental, physical, spiritual or emotional) of others.

Quilting humbles me, reminding me of how much I have and even how much I am. How do I respond to the 23 year-old woman who is gifted one of my quilts when she says, "Is it homemade? I've never had anything homemade before." And I think: What about macaroni necklaces, crayon drawings and notes that say "I love you mommy." Can this friendship braid with minkee back — something to snuggle with as she goes through stem cell transplants — ever console her, knowing she may not survive, let alone have children?

My teenage dream was to join the Peace Corps and help those less fortunate. Through quilting I am accomplishing this in a roundabout way. My quilts head to many different foreign countries, orphanages, medical facilities, and military hospitals. And within the USA, my quilts head to comfort those dealing with natural disasters such as hurricanes, tornadoes, and fires, as well as to hospitals located within the States.

I have stood by my husband's elbow as he learns to quilt as well. I have learned patience and celebrate his joy when he completes a project. And when we have visitors, he drags out the lap quilts he has made and proudly shares his works of art.

Indeed, I am humbled. I love being a part of the quilting sisterhood, and I don't even own my own quilt.

Grief Therapy

by **Tina Wright**
Mesa, Arizona

As a little girl, my mother had been taught to sew by her maternal grandmother. She adored her grandma Jean, and was the only granddaughter who took to the needle arts with a natural ability. While my mother was engaged to be married, my great-grandma Jean was in the process of making a Wedding Ring quilt when she fell and broke her hip. The quilt top was pieced but never quilted. The quilt sat in my mom's cedar chest and was never finished. Decades later when I was to be married, my sweet mama hired someone to quilt that pieced top for my wedding. Her gift to me was unspeakably dear, for it represented four generations of maternal love.

My mom passed away on Mother's Day 2001. She had just celebrated her 60th birthday. I grieved. I cried and mourned and wandered mindlessly through my days. I was inspired by my great-grandmother's quilt and decided that I was going to learn how to do that. I would

This is the first quilt I made, which I worked on to occupy my mind during those first months of grief after losing my mom at age 60. We had always said that we would learn quilting "someday." So I learned for the both of us.

learn how to make beautiful quilts and fill them with enough love to continue what my great-grandma Jean had begun. Quilting was the final frontier, so to speak, that my mom and I had planned to explore together. I needed this distraction to occupy my thoughts and days in a constructive way.

I bought a magazine that boasted a beautiful quilt on the cover which spoke to my heart. I looked up the address of a quilt store and drove into the city to begin my grief therapy. When I arrived there, I confessed that I knew zero about this art and that I would require some assistance. I gathered fabrics so beautiful and calming that they made my heart throb with joy. The ladies in the store showed me some of the quilt tops on display and gave me tips on ironing the seams in opposing directions, etc. By this time, they were aware of my mom's passing, and my need to focus my thoughts on something uplifting. They were so kind! That was the first day I felt the love and connection of The Sisterhood of Quilters.

Our family made a move out west in 2004. I was afraid that in my new hometown I would not find the same acceptance and inclusiveness I had experienced as a newbie. As soon as I went to church, I sought out the quilting crowd. I knew I would find what I was looking for there. How do you suppose I felt when woman after woman I asked gave me a blank stare?! I decided I had to teach these ladies about the Sisterhood, so I started a quilt group of my own and taught these gals what had been taught to me.

And so it goes on. My two daughters are quilting in their respective cities and circles. I feel my mom smiling down from heaven. I don't mourn my loss quite so much. I feel her all around me as I'm wrapped up in her grandmother's quilt.

Ladies of the Evening

by **BARB JANSEN**
Mashpee, Massachusetts

Twenty-five years ago I saw a quilt that I loved. I decided to learn to quilt simply because I couldn't afford to buy the hand-appliquéd, hand-quilted quilt, and I decided that it would be more fun to learn if I had some friends to quilt with.

I put an ad in the local free paper and invited people that were interested in quilting to come to my house. One woman came with her husband waiting in the car. He was concerned this could be a plot by an ax murderer to lure victims!

We started the group that night. Several women came and we helped each other learn with cardboard templates and scissors! Most everything was done by hand.

As my son grew and became a teenager, meeting at my house just wasn't as relaxing. We moved the group to the local community center.

Most of the regular members of "The Ladies of the Evening." From left to right: Jean Moore, Charlotte McCabe, Mary Gototweski, Barb Jansen, Marge Mignosa, Carol D'Angelo, Fran Tobio, Nan Chute, Mary Marty, Barb Bianchi. In front, Jackie Johnson, Florence Porzio. Absent members, Rosemarie Paliotto, Peggy Chambers, Kathie Porteous, Karen Burke.

We had been trying to think of a name, and still hadn't settled on one. One night, one of the members (the same one whose hubby thought I was an ax-murderer) called the community center to say we wouldn't be meeting that week. The person in charge of the schedule said "Are you the ladies that meet in the daytime?"

"No," she said, "we are the ladies of the evening." And so we had a name!

The "Ladies of the Evening" have met every Wednesday night for over 25 years. We have anywhere from 12 to 15 members and we have become the best of friends. We range in age from 50 to 90. One of our members that is almost 90 is one of the most prolific quilters that we have.

We have been through everything together. There have been deaths of children, grandchildren, and husbands. There have been divorces and other tragedies. When we attended the funeral of one of our members as a group, can you imagine the looks in the congregation when the priest said: "Doris was a long time Lady of the Evening?!"

We share our techniques, our fabric and our tools. But most of all, we share our lives, and quilt through it all. I never knew how my life would be changed by putting that ad in the paper, but I am very glad that I did!

The Fabric of My Life

by **HOLLY DUMONT**
San Martin, California

I learned to quilt in 1975. It was the year I started college and I was alone, in a new town without family or friends. Lonely, I wandered into a fabric store. Somehow, looking at patterns and fondling fabric made me feel less lost. In the back of the shop there was a quilt class going on. I was too shy to join, but managed to hang very close while the shop owner explained the entire process of getting started.

At the end of the class, the shop owner came over to where I was pretending to peruse Vogue patterns and handed me the pattern of the quilt the class was making. She thought I looked like I might need to quilt. Being a poor college student, I accepted the free pattern and went home to try it out. Of course I didn't have the right kind of fabric and couldn't afford to buy any, so I proceeded to make my first quilt out of leftover prom dress satin. It was a disaster, but while I was working on it, I wasn't alone.

In 1985, I found myself in the middle of a very ugly divorce. Once again, I couldn't go home. One evening I stumbled into a quilt shop. They were getting ready to start a beginning quilting class. I signed up there and then. I found myself three nights a week in a safe environment with no fears. And holy cow had quilting changed! There were rotary cutters and a riot of fabrics and patterns, new and old. Dozens of quilts later, the divorce was finally over and I was able to go from my job to my new home without worries.

I met a wonderful man, and by the 90s we were married with a child on the way. My husband loves quilts and bought me a new sewing machine and more fabric than I can sew in this lifetime. Through all the years, quilting has seen me through my troubles. On a bad day, I sort scraps. It reminds me how lucky I am that quilting became the fabric of my life.

The Grandma Quilt

by **ALISA GROVER SIMPSON**
Layton, Utah

I have always wanted to be able to create things that are beautiful and useful. Growing up, I learned to embroider and crochet, and enjoyed making projects for myself and others. After I was married, my husband's grandmother took me under her wing and taught me how to quilt. I loved the quiet contemplation and peace it afforded me. I love to make quilts, big and small. I have made them for friends and family, big enough for a queen sized bed and small enough for a doll. It has always been fun and relaxing, but recently it became more to me than that.

About two months ago my mother was diagnosed with cancer. She was going to have to go through the difficulty of chemotherapy, and I wanted her to have something that she could take with her to symbolize the love and support of her seven children and eleven grandchildren. I turned to quilting. I had all of my siblings send me hand prints of their kids, and I embroidered them on the quilt in their favorite colors. The

Photo Courtesy Alisa Grover Simpson

quilt had the name of each child and grandchild and in the middle was emblazoned our family motto during this difficult time, "Be Strong." This quilt was able to keep her warm and as comfortable as was possible during her first round of chemo. That would be its only trip with my mom to chemo. Devastatingly, she passed away only a few short weeks after the quilt was completed.

Before she died, my mom stated very clearly that she wanted the quilt left in her home for any of her grandchildren who visited to wrap up in and know that it was a "hug from Grandma." Her chemo quilt has become the Grandma Quilt, and was used often in those first few days after she left us. Quilting gave me the comfort of being useful and productive when there was nothing I could do to help my mom. In turn, it gave my mom a way to leave a token of her love behind with us when she passed.

Small World

---

by **STANISLAVA STRAKOVÁ**
Špačince, Slovakia

I'm Stanislava from Slovakia. I'm 38 in April and I'm teaching English at elementary school. My pupils love to play games and do activities connected with your language. One day I was looking for some interesting games for the lesson on the internet. I wanted to join teaching with some creative artwork for kids.

I was "surfing" the YouTube and "by accident" I clicked on Jenny's tutorial. I forgot everything about the teaching for the next day and spent hours (till the early morning) watching another and another video.

I was so amazed not only with the great pieces of work which Jenny was showing, but as a teacher, the enthusiastic way she was explaining to do things.

The next day I had to share with my older pupils one of the tutorials and let them translate what they understood into the Slovak language.

I was so surprised, that every one of my teens were watching the screen on the wall with open mouths and there was total silence in the classroom. Everybody wanted to catch Jenny's every word and to outrun the others, to be the first to explain how to do that. For some children, to study foreign language is not easy at all, but this day also my "slower" pupils could tell the others what she was telling about.

Later I realized that her art is to give people instructions about such complicated work — how to sew a quilt — in the easiest way it can be, so I knew, I CAN DO IT WITH HER.

I have to say, I have never ever sewn with a sewing machine in my life. But I went to the attic and brought down the historic, one hundred year-old sewing machine and did my first baby quilt, The Jelly Roll Race.

Everybody liked it and this was the time I fell in LOVE with sewing and quilting. I've bought an older "second hand" machine and I'm doing cushions, quilts, table runners, and bags for me and my family and friends. They all love my works. I ordered the great precuts from MSQC and the quilts and bags made of these were the prettiest.

Now I'm a passionate quilter and I'm saving money to buy a real BERNINA machine. This is what I'm looking forward to, this is my secret wish. I know, I'm as a five-year-old girl waiting for the best present under the Christmas tree, but these are the magic expectations in our lives.

And it's funny, but my students often say, "Mrs. Teacher, could we do some patchwork instead of learning?" I promised them to have our famous "quilting week" at the end of the school term in summer and I hope we will do some special patchwork poster on the wall, where every one of them can have their own piece of art.

I'm sending you the best wishes from Slovakia.

With love,
Stanislava

On Their Beds Lay Homemade Quilts

by **CECILY D.**
Bloomington, Illinois

W hen I was a baby, my mom made me a quilt. It was embroidered and hand quilted: ducks playing with a beach ball on a yellow background. It was a sign of her love for me. The quilt went with me to sleepovers and to camp. I cuddled it when I was sick and wore it like a cape. I kept that quilt on my bed until it was so threadbare that it couldn't handle the rough and tumble life of a high school student. It went into my special box.

Shortly thereafter, I received as a graduation present the Grandma's Flower Garden quilt my great-aunt was working on before she died of appendicitis at seventeen during the Depression. Verla Mae's quilt showed her hope of overcoming dust storms and financial setbacks to create beautiful things for the world to come. I needed to learn how to do what she was doing, so I picked up paper templates and tried to figure it out.

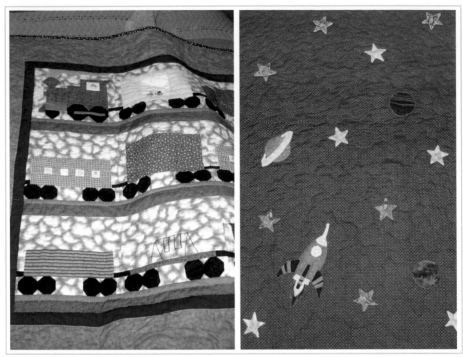

My two youngest boys' quilts. The space one was completed in 2012 and the train one was completed in 2010.

After my younger sister married, we took a quilt class together. Every week, I would drive the hour to her apartment, and then we'd sit through class, browse through the shop, and chat on the back steps before we separated for the week — me to grad school, her to a new baby. We hurried to finish our quilts for the show at the end and helped each other along.

When our brother left home, we pieced a quilt for him and pulled the whole family together to quilt it. The frame stood in my parents' living room for a long weekend, and when it was time for him to get on the airplane, his quilt went with him.

When my first baby came, my husband and I designed and made him a quilt. It was very simple: green frogs on a blue and purple background. But like my quilt, it sits on his bed. It is getting a little threadbare in spots, but it provides more than a physical warmth. It is a testimony of our love for him. It is the assurance of our hope for the future. He and his younger brothers will go forward into an uncertain future, but they will not be alone. At their side stand loved ones, seen and unseen. And on their beds lay homemade quilts.

From Your Mother and Me

by **CAROLYN RIDGE-LARSEN**
Romoland, California

My husband, John, and I were married while we were in our forties, a second marriage for both of us. John's first wife, JoAnn, passed from cancer. She was only 46 and left five children at home. John's oldest son married while we were dating. His daughter moved out on her own shortly after her brother's wedding. But his son Steven was away on a church mission when his mother passed. He had only been away a week and he decided to stay, saying that his mother would want it that way. Steven did not get a chance to mourn like the rest of his family and returned 2 years later to find his father engaged to a stranger he had never met. My relationship with Steven was strained, to say the least. All of John's children missed their mother terribly. It was hard for them to have another woman move into their mother's home.

I began cleaning out closets in the house and found boxes of material, quilting supplies, patterns, quilting frames, etc. I had never learned how

Photo Courtesy Carolyn Ridge-Larsen

to sew, let alone quilt, and I started giving away most of the items. Many projects had been started and never finished. Then one day I found a box of quilt squares. When I asked John about them, he said his wife had belonged to a quilting group and he thought they made a different square each month. Many of the squares were already put together while others were cut out and in individual bags. JoAnn had done a very good job with the squares, so I decided to keep this box, although I did not know what I was going to do with it.

A couple years later, Steven announced he was getting married. I was drawn to that box of quilt squares that JoAnn had started and decided I would put them together as a gift from his mother and myself. (My grandmother had given me a quilt when I got married many years before and I loved it more than anything because of the labor of love that went into putting it together.)

A dear friend and I spent endless hours finishing up the squares. She taught me how to finish the sashing, then we laid them out on the floor, sewed them together, put a border on and quilted. I did not tell anyone except my husband what I was doing so it would be a surprise. At the reception on the evening of the wedding, our gift was the last to be opened. The label read, "From your mother and me." There were not many dry eyes in the room, and Steven and his wife were very appreciative to have something from his mother.

Since that time over 20 years ago I have had the quilting bug. I have taken a few classes here and there. Then when I retired in 2010, I started looking online for beginning quilting classes and ran across MSQC. Now I have a sewing/quilting/craft room all to myself. I have made several baby quilts and I am currently quilting a lap quilt. With 26 grandchildren and 4 great grandchildren, I will be happily quilting for a very long time.

Welcome to the Club

by **BETHANY MARTINI**
Bellingham, Washington

My name is Bethany. I am 18 years old and I love to make quilts. I recently discovered this passion of mine last summer when I decided to make a quilt for myself to use in my dorm room at college. And boy, I am so glad I decided to do that!

I got out my mom's old sewing machine and started stitching. I had forgotten most of what I learned in my home economics class in middle school, so I used social media. Through Google and YouTube, I discovered the Missouri Star Quilt Co. and watched Jenny's video tutorials. Jenny made sewing and quilting look so easy and simple; I knew it was something I needed to try.

I started with a wall hanging and a table runner, and then I moved on to bed-size quilts. I have made seven quilts since July and I am so incredibly thankful to have found my passion. It is amazing to make something so beautiful and intricate from some fabric and thread.

I find it so funny to see my friends' faces when I tell them that I quilt.
I used to believe that quilting was something for grandmothers, but it
isn't! Yes, I am usually the youngest person at my local quilt store, and I
am fine with that!

I love how I am able to create something that is completely unique
and different. I love how I now buy new fabric instead of new clothes
or shoes. But most of all, I love how I am now part of this amazing
quilting community.

Still Serving

by **CINDY DAUGHERTY**
Lenexa, Kansas

I have sewn practically my whole life, beginning with making Barbie doll clothes with my sisters, on to clothing for myself and children, and now quilting. Prior to my "awakening," I believed it silly to cut up yards of fabric into squares and triangles and then sew all those pieces back together again.

And then it happened. I became disabled from chemical exposures during the first Gulf War. Unable to work, I had to find something to do that would occupy my mind and hands as a means to overcome the depression and anxiety of losing my military career.

I first began smocking, making my granddaughters beautiful dresses. Then my grandsons became jealous, having no "treasure" made special for them by their Nana. So I decided to start cutting up fabric in squares and triangles to make the boys quilts. The girls outgrew the dresses, so I gave up the smocking to become a full-time quilter.

My self-taught hobby became lasting therapy! Having very little money to spend on fabric, fellow quilters give me their scraps and I "dumpster dive" in the clearance bins at every store that sells fabric, always finding a treasure or two for a future project.

I make quilts for local charities, serving the poor, believing that many have fallen on hard times and need a little comfort and joy to overcome their situation. I make quilts for people who I believe inspire others, recognizing that many work long hours with little pay. I make quilts for children who are sick, believing there is a magical healing process that emanates from quilts. I make quilts for charity raffles hoping that someone will be more generous in their donations if there is a prize. Lastly, I make quilts for no reason, asking God to tell me who needs the quilt the most. And of course, everyone in my family has at least two quilts each, one silly and one serious.

Quilting brought me out of the "pity party" black hole that often occurs when people face life-changing situations. I'm often reminded of a quote from the movie *The Shawshank Redemption*: "Get busy living or get busy dying." I chose to be a survivor, recognizing that my disability could be a lot worse, as so many Gulf War vets died from the exposure, while others are more severely injured than myself.

I no longer have "bad days" because I have designated them as "resting days" in preparation for the next project. Quilting will never cure the damages my body sustained, but it has made it possible for me to recognize something greater. It's in giving that we each receive the bounty of God's love and mercy. I didn't retire from active duty, I simply enlisted in God's quilting army, sewing squares and triangles together for others to receive.

Remembering Vets With Quilts

by **PAM WALLACE**
Douglasville, Georgia

A few years ago, a friend of mine began a tour of duty in Afghanistan. After being there for a few weeks, he posted photos on Facebook that showed him standing in front of a khaki-colored building, surrounded by nothing but sand and more sand. The barren landscape gave me the idea to brighten his day by sending him a colorful quilt. Since I work a full-time job and don't have a lot of time for quilting, I asked my mother (a long-time quilter) if she had any colorful quilts that she would be willing to part with, and she gave me one that I shipped to my soldier friend in Afghanistan. He quickly sent my mother back a thank-you note, along with his Army medallion that he was given when he joined the Army. My mother carries that medallion with her everywhere, proudly showing it to friends and family! And this is where a mission of love began among a few good quilting friends.

It's remarkable how a simple act of kindness can make everyone

Salem St. James (left), an Army medic, sent this picture to the quilters after receiving the quilt.

involved feel appreciated, both the giver and the receiver, as we had seen with the first quilt that we sent to my soldier friend. We sent the quilt to him just to brighten his life, and to cover him in the warmth of our love while he was in Afghanistan, but we were the ones that got the biggest blessing! Because the quilt we gave him made him so happy, it encouraged us to begin plotting a mission of love for another soldier.

I told a good friend and coworker of mine this story and she wanted in on the action! The three of us share a love of quilting, and also share a love for our soldiers. My brother had served in Desert Storm, my coworker's son-in-law is currently a U.S. military chaplain in Germany, and my mother married my dad, a retired-military-veteran. We decided to parlay our passion into a gift that would make another soldier feel appreciated and came up with a name for our mission: the Soldier-Quilt-Love-Quest.

We wanted to send our second quilt to a female soldier in Afghanistan, so we began working on it immediately! I hand-embroidered the hearts on the blocks, my coworker and I designed and machine-pieced the quilt top together, and my mother and I hand-quilted the quilt. Then, we sent the finished quilt to a military hospital in Afghanistan with instructions that it be delivered to a woman soldier. It ended up in the arms of an Army medic named Salem St. James. Salem loved the quilt and quickly thanked us in an email. The picture she attached in her email surprised all of us, as we had no idea Salem was a medic, or that our design would resemble the red cross emblem you see on her medic helicopter.

Once again, we, the givers, received the biggest blessing in knowing that our gift for someone else ended up right where it was supposed to go. Both soldiers have since come back home safely, and both soldiers have sent us emails telling us that those quilts are still constant reminders of how important it was to feel love and appreciated, especially while in a barren land surrounded by war and hate.

We hope to send at least one quilt each year to a U.S. soldier deployed in a war zone. It is truly a blessing to me to know that my mother, a daughter of a quilter, and a quilter most of her life, has passed her quilting legacy onto me, and that I share that same love for quilting with many other quilting friends. Quilting is truly a gift that keeps on giving, and blesses the quilters most of all!

And so, we are working on our next mission of love to create another quilt for a U.S. soldier, and the Soldier-Quilt-Love-Quest (SQLQ) continues.

The Making of a Quilter

✳

by **EILEEN M. CULLINANE**
Warwick, Rhode Island

I t was a dark and stormy night. After drinking one half of a spirited beverage, I agreed to learn how to quilt. My friend, Sue, having over thirty years of quilting experience, would teach me. Turning me into a quilter would be like trying to turn Don Knotts into Mr. America. But we were up for the challenge. Why not learn something new in my late fifties?

So Sue taught me how to quilt on her old Singer Featherweight. I loved everything about it: fabric and color selection, stitching quarter inch seam after quarter inch seam, the machines, all the clever tools of the trade, and, most importantly, the camaraderie!

We founded our own club: The "Sew-Sew" Quilting Club of Rhode Island - Southern Chapter. We have three members. I am the Supreme Commander For Life (SCFL). Sue is Chief Advisor. Our friend, Laurie, is

a member. Together we have quilted some special gifts for family and friends! (Even the dog got a little disappearing nine patch.)

I went on eBay in search of my own sewing machine. I emailed Sue, telling her I purchased a Featherweight sewing machine for fifty dollars! She checked the website and emailed me back. "I think you just bought a case." She was right. The mailman delivered an empty sewing machine case. (That's why she is Chief Advisor.)

Anyway, as you can see, quilting has changed my life in many ways. Here are just two examples: First, my friends have banned me from shopping on eBay, and secondly, I can literally leave my friends and family in stitches!

Sewn With Love and Tears

by **JACKIE (HURD) LIVINGSTON**
Nashua, Iowa

My father passed away in 2002 from prostate cancer. Before he passed, I would take him and my mother for his treatments and I would often have to help him in the clinic, as he would get so tired.

I always teased him about his flashy briefs: red polka dots, purple paisleys, teal swirls, etc. I asked him what nurses he was trying to impress! He would always laugh with that twinkle in his eye.

After Dad passed away and Mom was ready to clean his closet, I told her I would take his things to Goodwill for her. But first, I pulled out all those briefs and some shirts. I started pillow-style: hand-pieced, 3" hexagon pieces from all those briefs and shirts for a Grandmother's Flower Garden quilt. I was a school bus driver at the time, so those pieces went to many sports activities over about a 6-month period.

Photo Courtesy Jackie Livingston

Well, I finally got it put together into that Grandmothers Flower Garden quilt. I named the quilt "Dad's Bloomers" and gave it to my Mother for her 80th birthday. She cried and said she had no idea I was doing this for her. It was wonderful therapy for me two-fold: therapy of remembering my dad and the laughs we had, plus therapy of thinking of the enjoyment Mother was going to get from that quilt. I made a label for the quilt that told the story of Dad and his fancy briefs.

The quilt now hangs in my home, as Mother also has passed. I still giggle at the thought of Dad and his briefs and Mom's tears of joy when receiving the quilt. Every stitch was sewn with love and tears.

Threadbare

by **BECKY PILAND**
Berryton, Kansas

I am a first generation quilter. In fact, I loved fibers as a preschooler and have spent years teaching myself to knit, crochet, needlepoint, and quilt. I began making quilts for family members for important events in their lives. About three years ago, I made a large throw for my niece when her son was born. It was deliberately made large so the entire family could snuggle together. As a parent, I understood the importance of holding your children as long and as often as possible because they grow so quickly.

Imagine my dismay when I learned that the quilt had been dragged on the floor and had the dog lay on it, not to mention the baby getting sick on it. After all, I had spent hours making the quilt. As the baby grew, he cried for his "night, night." His parents would frantically wash and dry it so he would go to sleep. He had to have it every night. The quilt was used when the baby suffered an asthma attack and when his father

recovered from injuries while serving our country in Afghanistan. The entire family loved the quilt and used it often. I pictured the quilt to be completely threadbare and stained, and was heartbroken.

Then, about a year ago I began to realize that the quilt was a gift and gifts are just that: given with no stipulations. If this quilt wore out, I'd make them another. My heart melted when my niece sent a picture of her little boy this December with the quilt wrapped over his head. It had been a tent, a hoodie and a turtle just that day. I could imagine this little guy as an adult telling his wife about all the childhood memories this quilt held.

Then the unthinkable happened. On January 31 of this year, my niece's husband (the little boy's dad) went down in a plane he piloted while working for the Arkansas Forestry Department. Countless people searched for 12 days. Unfortunately, he did not survive. However, when I was at my niece's home, I saw the quilt folded on the couch right where they could snuggle together and comfort each other as they mourn the loss of their loved one.

Quilts are made with love and given in love with no strings attached. I used to think that something that took so much time and money should remain museum quality, but I have finally realized it's a bigger honor to have a quilt used by the recipient because they love it and know it was given to them in love.

Quilting Heritage

by **KIM BELL**
Arlington, Texas

Several years (ok, decades!) ago I became a genealogy enthusiast when, as a teenager, I placed flowers on graves of my ancestors in Iowa with my grandparents on "Decoration Day." At each grave site, I was regaled again with stories, some familiar, some not so, some funny, some sad, and a few tragic.

Like my great-great-great grandmother who was killed by a lightning strike in the 1870s while hanging laundry on the line, leaving behind a husband and seven little children. Was she hanging quilts that she made? I wonder. Her story captivated me: she and her husband immigrated from Ireland separately, somehow met and fell in love in New Jersey and made their way west to become farmers. Landowners! They were Irish Catholic farmers in a time when that was a difficult thing to be. Standing at her grave I cheered for her, her husband, and their children from so far in the future I wasn't even a thought in her mind.

One of my great grandmother's quilts, made in the 1930s. To us it is a masterpiece that we all love.

They began a heritage of farming the land that continues to this day in my family.

Like my great-great grandmother who, with her husband and children, came to Iowa from Illinois in a covered wagon. She was known as "the quilter" in our family. She raised her large family at the turn of the 1900s. She created quilts before there was electricity, long before precuts and rotary cutters. She lost three small children to the Spanish Flu, and I imagine that she comforted those sick babies with her softest quilts during their illness. I imagine that because I know she made sure each of her children, grandchildren, and great grandchildren had a hand-pieced, hand-sewn and hand-quilted masterpiece before she died at the age of 96, shortly before the moon landing. She and her husband, too, were farmers, and I marvel at all they saw in their lifetime, from covered wagons to rocket ships. They lived in a time that was quintessentially American.

Like my own mother (who began quilting so that each of her grandchildren were cuddled in their own baby quilts made by her) I came late to the quilting table, but I knew that I wanted to continue the heritage of quilting handed to me by my mother, who at that time was battling terminal cancer. The Christmas quilt we worked on together, my first and her last, is an heirloom that I treasure; it rightly has a central place in my Christmas decorations.

When I am in my craft room at my sewing machine I am never alone. Somehow in the rhythm of stitching, and as pieces are joined together, I am connected to my mother and grandmothers. My thoughts are full and I find such comfort, therapy really.

Quilting connects me to my roots, to a family heritage and in small part to the American experience.

Two Sides to Every Story

by **KIM and JEAN CREAMER**
Omaha, Nebraska

I started quilting at a young age. My grandmother taught me to quilt when I was ten and I have been quilting off and on for several years until recently. Now I have a long arm quilting machine and have been quite productive since.

I quilt because I enjoy taking a pattern and picking out fabric that I feel will make the quilt personal to the one I am planning on giving it to. I love seeing the happiness it brings when they see the quilt I made especially for them. I have been blessed by God in order to be a blessing to others. I get such a great reward when I see their faces light up at the sight of their new quilt. Quilting allows me to be creative and create a one-of-a-kind product that can not be found at any store. The Bible says to think of others as more important than yourself.

Scraaaatch all that! This is the husband talking. I will give you the real reason why she is into quilting. She uses quilting as an excuse in order to avoid me at night. It's an avoidance technique. While she is buffing her halo I will fill you in on the "rest of the story." She has been using quilting to avoid quality time with me. She says she will "be right up" after she does an 8 block jelly roll and rewinds her bobbin. Baloney! With a bobbin the size of a full length movie reel there is no way she'll "be right up."

Slowly I doze off. The alarm wakes me up and I ask her, "Where were you?" She says, "Sleeping." I say, "Why didn't you wake me up?" She says, "I tried." I say, "Try harder!" Useless arguing ... once again I'm out-foxed by the Quilting Queen of the tundra.

Fabric must be catnip for quilters. She can't go anywhere without fabric in her hands. When she is not quilting she is knitting constantly; at home, on road trips. She even made knitting needles out of plastic in order to sneak them past the airport metal detectors so she can knit on the plane. No one said a word — amazing (Don't tell the FAA — our little secret!)

It's getting worse. If she wasn't already cold enough she now wants to go on a quilting cruise to ... Alaska. So much for global warming.

Signed: Freezer Burned in Omaha

Out of the Ashes

by **RITA JACKSON**
Philo, Illinois

My mother was the quilter in the family, and a darn good one at that. Unfortunately, she was tortured with mental illness most of her life and often her struggles were reflected in her quilts in little ways. Not-so-pleasant childhood memories could be elicited from just looking at some of her work.

While cleaning out the garage five years ago, I stumbled across a long-forgotten tattered box. Opening it, I discovered 85 quilt blocks that Mom (now deceased) had cut out and embroidered based on Sun-Bonnet Sue. The fabrics were pieces that had been sewn or worn by my grandmother, my mother, my sister and me. A quilted story of four generations! Some pieces triggered difficult memories in our lives, others, good times. But what was I going to do with them? I was NOT a quilter.

My daughter, Kim Leman, with her quilt.

I contacted a small quilting circle at a local Methodist church for help. Long story short, over the ensuing three years these precious ladies quilted three unique twin quilts out of the blocks which were later given to my daughters and niece.

I will always remember when my neighbor and co-quilter, Martha, who let me take a peek at the almost-finished first quilt at church one day. As she unrolled the protective covering on the quilt, I stood there and cried.

I remember thinking, "Out of the ashes has come this beautiful treasure." When my niece received her quilt, both my sister and I stood and cried.

My quilting family invited me to start quilting with them, and since that time I have been hooked! I was blessed to help quilt the last two of the three quilts. Last summer, I was invited by the group to go on a two day shop-hop. Like a tried and true quilter, I spent way too much money and had a blast!

I have been a special education teacher for almost 30 years and I retired in June this year. What do I have planned for retirement? Among other things, I am opening a little quilt studio in the mountains of North Carolina.

A New Lease on Life

by **NANCY SILVERMAN**
Riverside, Rhode Island

At 50, I had never crafted anything by hand. We lived in Macau, where I taught at a university, and since I was teaching full time I didn't really have time nor interest in crafting. When my husband, Charles, fell ill, we moved to Rhode Island so he could have the medical care he needed. After several major surgeries, it was clear I had to leave my job and take care of him at home. The alternative was for Charles to be in a nursing facility, which was not really an option for us.

That's when I had the opportunity to open the box where my wedding present, a Janome DC3050, had been sitting unused for many years. I didn't really know what to do nor how to start doing anything until a friend, Sandy, came with a bagful of scraps. Sandy showed me how to piece scraps together and make a block. Then she taught me how to join the blocks. Sandy's husband, Joe, gave one of his kidneys to my husband, Charles, in a transplant done some 13 years ago. Joe's kidney

gave Charles a new lease on life and Sandy's quilting lessons did the same for me.

Charles was so ill that I had to stay up most of the night, monitoring his breathing and administering medication every hour. I slept some during the day when there were nursing aides to help us. I survived the stressful, long nights piecing scraps together and making more blocks. Sandy brought some quilting books and magazines where I learned different quilt patterns. Best of all, I found the MSQC website where I have been buying most of my quilting supplies while also learning more techniques via Jenny Doan's tutorials on YouTube! I have learned how to quilt-as-you-go and even appliqué. The nightly quilting frenzy enabled me to make dozens of quilted adult bibs, walker totes, wheelchair ponchos, lap and even full-sized quilts that were all given away to handicapped elderly in similar situations as my husband.

Nowadays, Charles is coping with his illness and managing wonderfully as he is recovering. Meanwhile, I have gotten used to quilting at night as I experiment and learn endless possibilities for quilting when it is quiet and peaceful. Quilting has undoubtedly changed my life as every project I finish eventually finds its way to someone who needs it, even if it is a bib to protect one's clothing at breakfast, a walker tote to carry one's medication around, or a wheelchair poncho to keep warm when going to a doctor's appointment. More recently, I boxed quilted blankets and sent them to victims of Superstorm Yolanda in the Philippines. I still quilt every night and right now I'm making shopping totes using precuts from MSQC. Viva la quilt!

A Hobby That Soothes the Soul

by **CHERYL CLINTON NELSON**
Mountain Home, Arkansas

I did random sewing projects for many years, making dresses for my daughter when she was little and a few clothes for myself when I got a more professional job. I just did it whenever the mood struck me and I was learning as I went. My mother is a wonderful seamstress and makes 98 percent of all her clothes, but somehow as a kid I never got interested.

What always tickled my fancy were quilts. I had books on quilts that were made in my home state of Arkansas, featuring quilts made by my great grandmother and great aunt. I just didn't have the courage to think I could actually make one of those beautiful creations — until November 1996, that is.

On a terrible night in November 1996 my husband and I received the phone call that no one wants to get: car accident, granddaughter in

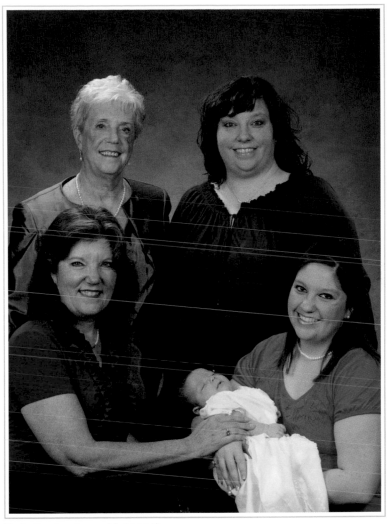

This is our most precious picture, a five-generation photo taken in 2013 when my great-granddaughter was born. Addison is wearing the Christening gown that my mother made by hand for me. Every baby in our family has worn that gown.

critical condition, may not make it through the night. She was four at the time.

Despite the odds, she survived, but was hospitalized for long weeks after she regained consciousness. She underwent physical and speech therapy, learned to walk again, and recovered from losing a kidney. This is when I took up quilting with a vengeance.

I bought a magazine with a Christmas quilt on the cover. I didn't have the time to order the kit and wait for it to arrive. I needed something right away to keep my hands busy while we waited. So I rifled through my stash of leftover scraps and set out to copy the quilt pattern as best I could. Through long nights on my shift sitting with my granddaughter, I would piece together little Christmas trees, Santas, snowmen, churches, and angels for the quilt squares. I invented some of own designs too. That quilt gave me purpose and focus and hope for my granddaughter's recovery.

And recover she did! Now she is a mother with a precious little daughter of her own. Every Christmas when I bring out that quilt, I hold it and say a silent prayer of thanks. My heart rejoices at the grace of God, and that quilt got me started on a hobby that soothes my soul to this day!

Quilting Through Cancer

by **WENDY GARNER**
Lapeer, Michigan

I started out sewing dresses and even making my wedding gown. When I became pregnant, I decided to make a quilt. The results were pretty hideous and I never finished it; just too intimidated to try again.

Raising a family while working kept me too busy to do much sewing. The birth of my first granddaughter started me sewing again - little dresses.

At the age of 48 I was diagnosed with breast cancer. Surgery, radiation, and chemo kept me from being there when my grandson was born. By the following January, I was diagnosed with breast cancer again - surgery and radiation this time, no chemo. Years went by with no recurrence of the cancer.

A friend started a machine embroidery group at our local senior center. I had been given an embroidery machine and really needed help understanding how to use it properly, so I joined the group. As more ladies joined the group, we realized that many of them were quilters. Soon there was more quilting being done than embroidery.

Another grandchild was on the way, so I took the plunge and made a flannel baby quilt. I was proud of that first quilt, small though it was. Encouraged, I started a castle quilt for my grandson and a kitten quilt for my oldest granddaughter. Another granddaughter was born and I started caring for her daily leaving no time to quilt. The castle and kitty quilts remained unfinished.

As my 60th birthday approached, extreme pain in my leg sent me from doctor to doctor. When I could no longer walk, I was taken by ambulance to the hospital. They discovered that breast cancer had eaten through my femur. I now had Stage 4 breast cancer.

No longer able to care for my granddaughter, I was broken hearted. I felt like I had lost my identity. After radiation, a second surgery on my leg, and monthly shots to strengthen my bones, I started sewing again.

A breast cancer awareness party drew me to start buying coordinating pink fabrics. The day of the party, my sister-in-law was diagnosed with throat cancer. A collector of pink flamingos, I knew the pink quilt was meant for her. I started embroidering flamingos for the quilt.

Spurred on by her illness, I finished the quilt in record time! I named the quilt, "In The Pink."

The long put-aside castle and kitten quilts needed to be finished, and fast. I had another operation scheduled, this time a knee replacement. I delivered the quilts at my granddaughter's fourth birthday party. The kitten quilt was no longer suitable for my 15 year-old granddaughter, so the birthday girl received it.

I am recuperating from my knee replacement and planning out a new quilt for my granddaughter's 15th birthday. She is a singer, so it will be a musical quilt, with a piano key border. After I finish that, another quilt will be due for my newest granddaughter, who will be two in July.

To Everything There is a Season

by **LINDA COOK**
Jerseyville, Illinois

My mother was a registered nurse and gave comfort to people all her life. It never seemed fair that her last four years were spent in a nursing home not knowing where she was or who family and friends were. Alzheimer's robs both individuals and families of so much.

A month after she went to live in the nursing home, I made a wall quilt. She loved it, so each season I would do a new one. Staff members and residents would come to her room to see her new quilt. She was very proud to show them off and always knew I made them for her. The last year I made one a month. We would hang them and talk about them. We made a connection to the end through quilts.

At the funeral staff members came by and said how sweet she was, how much they would miss her and how much they would miss her quilts. She always loved them so.

Channeling Grandma

*

by **EMILY DAVIDSON MANN**
Merrick, New York

My grandmother, a naturalized U.S. citizen, was a dressmaker by trade since childhood. Her skills and talents nurtured her children through the Great Depression. She taught me by age eight to crochet, knit, hand sew, embroider, and needlepoint. She taught me tricks of her trade, and bought me a cabinet-style Singer sewing machine in 1962, which my mother thought was insanely extravagant for a teenager. My grandma's heavily accented English retort was, "I know my granddaughter, she will sew."

That granddaughter did sew! The heavy machine still works, forward and back, no fancy stitches. It followed me through college, graduate school, several apartments, a house, and two children; but just for sewing, never quilting.

In 2003, a quilter friend told me, "You can sew and you love jig-saw puzzles, you should quilt."

I said, "Too messy, too much work, all the tools, measuring and cutting, and I have no work space."

But every time my friend displayed her next gorgeous quilting creation, telling me, "You can do this, you know," I would contemplate the colors, patterns, shapes, illusions, and textures. I finally bought a beginner's quilting book and learned how to audition, compare, contrast, and combine various scale prints. I made my first project, a 9-block sampler with a pinwheel, bow tie, bear paw, drunkard's path, Ohio star, fence rail, honey bee, basket, and 9-patch hearts. It wasn't perfect, but admirable.

Quilting is now my go-to craft for gifting occasions, as well as refreshing my own home decor. It can be quick or slow. No work space? The dining room table holds projects in myriad stages of planning or completion. My grown son's bedroom houses my stash and tools. I consult my artist daughter for color options.

On a trip to southern France in 2007, I bought Provençal fabrics to jump-start a souvenir gift to myself, still awaiting an appropriate border and finishing touches. Online, I collect patterns and bookmark tutorials, create wish lists, and search for sales, short cuts, and inspiration. I joined a local quilt guild and read quilt magazines while waiting for doctors appointments.

Photo Courtesy Emily Davidson Mann

I surprised my mother with a queen size fence rail designed from 1930s reproductions reminiscent of her childhood. She asked, "How did you do all this?" and I replied, "I channeled Grandma."

Quilting? Too messy, needs work space. No problem. I am a quilter.

Finding Courage

by **CINDY HARRIS**
Northport, Alabama

A couple of years ago, I finally got the courage to leave an abusive husband of ten years. Unless a person has had a lesson in why victims of domestic violence stay in that relationship, most people do not understand. I stayed until my body could not handle it anymore.

The last night of abuse, the police told me that they had been called to my house so many times that time was running out on me. They said that each call they got to go to my address they really believed that instead of just my husband leaving in the back of a patrol car, I would be leaving in a body bag. Every time, I had him arrested and then foolishly bailed him out of jail and went back.

After I finally left, I decided I needed to do something to keep my mind busy. I was always fascinated with quilts, always drawn to them at fairs and people's homes. I decided to buy fabric and a sewing machine and just start quilting. I have never had anyone in my family teach me anything about sewing or quilting, so I'm not sure why I have always been so attracted to the idea of it.

I started sewing and quilting fabric but my quilts were not very good, as I did not know what I was doing. I eventually got on the internet and went to YouTube and searched quilting. Jenny Doan was one of the videos

Photo Courtesy Cindy Harris

that came up. I watched her videos all evening and was hooked. She made so much sense and I was having those "aha" moments. I realized too why my quilts didn't look right. I started watching from the very beginning of the Missouri Star Quilt Company videos and watched every one of them not once, not twice, but at least three times. I started ordering my materials online from MSQC and it has been so much fun!

Since I really learned how to piece and quilt, I have made so many quilts for my children and other family members. I have quilted around 20 quilts in the last year and I still do not have one of my own. I am working on one now that I am keeping for myself. I have just recently learned to make pictures with fabric and I am working on one which depicts how much domestic violence hurts. I am really excited about it, The quilting has been so therapeutic to me emotionally.

Now I can touch others' lives by creating something very special just for them and giving it to them. Giving gives me so much pleasure.

Hooked on a New Hobby

by **SANDRA**
Giessen, Germany

There have been a long, dark period (42 years) in my life when I did not know anything about quilting or quilts.

I live in Germany and we use duvets and woolen blankets. Of course I had seen patchwork, but in most cases the pattern is printed right onto the fabric.

Then, in October 2013, we visited the parents of our exchange students. In their home we had a bed with a quilt (the first I ever touched!) and I fell in love with this piece made of little patches of fabric. While staying in America, I searched for a quilt to take home. But two weeks had been too short a time - we wanted to see the land and meet people - so I did not find a quilt. And in addition, our suitcases were too small for carrying one in a good size.

Back in Germany I tried to buy a quilt here, but the variety was terrifying little, only simple squares stitched together! Then I tripped over one of Jenny's tutorial, and a second, and a third.... After watching nearly all of them, I got so excited and confident that I was sure I would make my own quilts. I started quilting in the middle of November, and on Christmas each of my three kids — and of course hubby and I — each had our own quilt!

Many cushions (as pattern samples) followed, and my last project has been a quilt for a friend with breast cancer in the hope to help fighting against her disease.

It makes so much fun to create with fabric and yarn that I have to admit that I am hooked on my new hobby!

Thank you for those great tutorials which let a German learn how to live like an American (at least a little bit!).

The Heirloom Singer

by **JOSIE SCHMUCKER**
Salem, Oregon

When she was eighteen, my great grandmother Rhoda came to America via a long boat ride from Scotland with her sister Nellie and the rest of her family. When she got to America she met and married my great grandpa and the rest is history!

Ever since my mother and her sisters were little, they remember sewing on Grandma Rhoda's sewing machine. Grandma Rhoda taught her daughter and granddaughters how to sew on that machine. It is a 1927 Singer Portable Electric Sewing Machine model 128-23 with a vibrating shuttle. My mom likes to think that Grandma Rhoda got it as a wedding gift. I like the thought of that too, so that is what I will stick with until I know the truth!

Fast forward to when my mom was closer to my age, 28. Grandma Rhoda gave this sewing machine to my Aunt, my Mom's younger sister.

For my mom who was the sewist in the family, this kind of hurt! She had loved this machine so much, and would have loved the opportunity to have it.

Now my Mom is almost 60 and she told me about this machine. Yes, I had not known about it till about five months ago!

I am a self-taught quilter and I love to stare at those antique Singers in the window at the antique shops, but have never gotten my hands on one. So I was ecstatic when she told me about this machine! Once she saw how excited I was, my Mom thought after all this time she might ask my aunt if she would be willing to pass it on. My aunt said: "Of course I will send it to you. I would LOVE for Josie to have it!" When Mom told me this I squealed like a little girl; I could hardly wait to see it and touch it and use it!

After some shipping issues and other fiascos the machine finally made its way from South Carolina to Oregon. It still has most of the original parts, and it even comes in the cutest little carrying case I have ever laid my eyes on. It looks like a wooden mailbox!

Through my local quilt guild I found a Singer sewing machine repair man and he jumped at the chance to repair and clean up my new heirloom machine. It didn't even take him a week and he had her all shined up and running like new. I couldn't believe it! To sit and sew at the same machine my great-grandmother, grandmother, aunts and mother sewed on is indescribable! I am forever blessed to have this in my possession and I hope that I have made my Great Grandmother Rhoda proud!

What He Doesn't Know Won't Hurt Him

by **PHYLLIS JAMISON MARCUS**
Surprise, Arizona

I n 1987 when my quilt addiction was in full possession of my brain, I knew there wasn't any more room in my house for fabric. I had taken to hiding fabric behind the walk-in bar (we weren't drinkers) and in the trunk of my fairly small Toyota Corolla. But things were getting harder to hide and my car was older in age.

I asked my husband if it was time for a new car for me and he agreed that it was. We went car shopping and I told him that I had fallen in love with the new Toyota Camry. He looked it over and we talked with the salesman. It was a done deal. However, my husband could not understand why I wouldn't take immediate delivery and leave my Corolla there. I said that I just wasn't quite ready to close the deal.

We drove home and I dropped him off. I drove over to my friendly quilt shop (Bearly Stitchin', Pasadena, CA) and unloaded several hundred yards of fabric, and then drove home. I then announced that I was ready to make the deal on the new car, but I could handle it on my own. (I wanted to be a very modern woman.) I went to the dealership, closed the deal, went to Bearly Stitchin' and loaded in all my fabric, (with room to spare) and drove home. It took a while, but he did discover that while I did not need a new car, I did need a new trunk!

The Magic Quilt

by **MARY LOU BIEDERMANN**
Shingle Springs, California

I taught myself to sew early, but was never a quilter. In the early
'80s I decided to try my hand at quilting a Mother's Day gift. I
went down to the local dime store and bought a yard each of varying
blues and made up my own quilt pattern (which looked just like today's
rail fence pattern). I cut each strip individually and sewed it all together.
My "quilting" was tied at each corner with yarn. I mailed it out and
of course my mother said she loved it. A few years later, Mom was
diagnosed with stomach cancer, so home I went.

During her treatments, she wanted nothing but that blue strip quilt. She
said it was like magic; whether she was warm or cold, the quilt was just
right. After she died, I took the quilt home with me.

Fast forward a few more years and my daughter only wanted the
"magic" quilt on her bed, so it became hers (and the dog's, cat's, doll's,

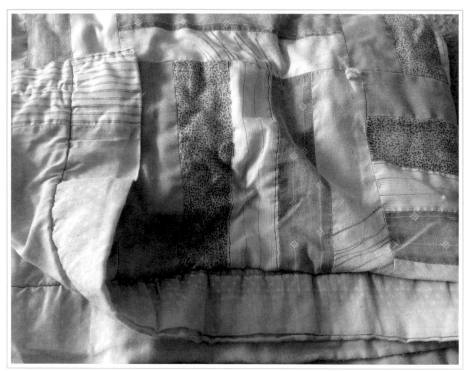

etc.). Here it is 30 years later, and that quilt still holds a place on my daughter's bed. It's been washed so many times, I'm pretty sure there isn't any batting left. But it doesn't look too bad folded up at the end of her bed. No, it doesn't look bad at all.

A Legacy of Love

by **TERESA LIVESAY MYERS**
Kansas City, Missouri

I am 60 years old and have a beautiful granddaughter, Emma, who is five and the most handsome grandson, Padraig, who is three. To say I am blessed is an understatement, I also have the most wonderful, patient, and understanding husband and three precious children. I must compliment my husband because he is always happy to accompany me to the Missouri Star Quilt Company. It's convenient for him to get a quick haircut next door, however he also enjoys browsing through the quilt shop watching we women go nuts over the beautiful fabric.

I was born to a sharecropper and his lovely wife. They worked side by side in the fields to earn a poor man's dollar in order to feed their five children. When winter came, Dad would hang Mom's quilting racks in the living room from the ceiling. Furniture would be rearranged in order to make room for the new fixture that would remain until cotton was up in the spring and ready to be chopped. As a sharecropper, Dad moved us frequently, always looking for more acreage. Each land owner had a house for us, always in disrepair and impossible to heat in the winter.

My mom's quilts back in those years weren't works of beauty, but quilts of necessity to protect her family from the biting cold of the night. Worn out jeans from my dad and three brothers were cut into scraps, pieced together and quilted to provide much needed protection from the freezing temperatures on those long winter nights when the fire would die low in the old wood-burning stove.

As years passed and Mom spent less time in the field, her quilts became pieces of art, works of love with every stitch. I recall one quilt in particular she made for me. I would sit in bed and pick out blocks she had taken from some old pajamas that once belonged to my sister and me, pieces from Mom's dresses, Dad's shirts, and many other special swatches that brought many happy thoughts. When she became a grandmother, quilts for the grandchildren started whirling from her machine, then quilts for her grown children and great grandchildren.

Mom is gone now, but she left behind a legacy of love for her family. Every hour she sat at her hanging quilt rack, back bent, sewing tiny precise stitches, was a labor of love. It was her heart's desire all throughout life to care for her family, making sure the basic needs were met: love, food and the warmth of a quilt sewn from border to border with love.

Mom, I have inherited your love for sewing, which I learned from sitting on your knee as you sewed, as well as your love for quilting. Regretfully, I have gotten a later start on my quilting skills than you, however, I am having fun and sewing every stitch with love.

Thank you, Mom, for loving me so very much. I cherish all the nights I had the honor to sleep underneath my quilt of love stitched by your sweet, soft hands. You would be very happy to know that I am teaching Emma, your great granddaughter, to sew and quilt.

It Happened on a Tuesday

by **JOANNE BLANTON**
Battle Ground, Washington

I was invited to speak at a women's retreat two years ago. During the afternoon free time, several of the women, probably a third of the group, jumped into cars together and took off in search of quilt shops. (I know these ladies now so don't kid yourself, they had a plan, and a map!) During the retreat I heard many of their life stories as well as a common thread (did I just say thread?), which was the fellowship of the Tuesday morning quilt and craft group that met at the church.

In the afterglow of the retreat I decided to attend the Tuesday group. Day one I took a knitting project I had been working on for two years (sigh). There were scrapbookers, embroiderers, card makers, beaders, knitters, and crocheters, and of course the quilters, plus sack lunches and love!

I began buying books. Quilting books. Lots of quilting books. Fat quarters? Jelly rolls? Layer cakes? Oh my! I began stalking quilt shops and finally purchased my first quilt project. It was out of a book and it was a sampler. I made that sampler without telling anyone and had it quilted, then took it in for show and tell. When I think of it now, I even laugh at myself, I spent waaaaaay too much money. Still, two years later, I have fabric from that project I'm using to quilt with! And I had the nerve to be proud of that quilt! Today, it's in a very special and cozy spot on the bottom of my linen closet. But you know what? My peeps (as I affectionately refer the Tuesday group) were proud of me too. They had a heads up on what had to be done if they were to turn me into a proper quilter!

But during the time I was working on that quilt, my daughter and daughters-in-law thought I was soooo clever. They wanted to quilt too. Out of that desire, the "Sista's Night" was born. On Thursday nights my daughter and daughters-in-law came over to my house. I made tapas and spirits, and the girls made quilts. One of our sons came upstairs one Thursday evening looking for his wife and said, "This looks like a sweatshop in here!"

We found sewing machines and fabric at yard sales. I remember one of my daughters-in-law calling me from a yard sale asking, "Is $2 a yard a lot to pay for fabric?" I answered, "Stay where you are, I'm coming to you!"

Even though I was out of town occasionally on a Thursday night, the Sista's still met. I received a call one of those nights and one of my daughters-in-law asked, "You know that little bobber thingy? Well its empty, how does it work to get thread on there?" I taught them to wind a bobbin remotely and I'd like to say I taught them to quilt, but YouTube, the dictionary, a lot of help from my peeps, and books (lots of quilting books) led us to eventually hanging seven quilts that first summer in the local quilt show.

But quilting is so very much more than acquiring a skill. Heart and soul get involved, friendships are forged, inspiration is abundant.

The other day I stopped for a moment to take in my Tuesday morning group. Scattered around several tables were groups of women from all walks, woven by a common thread (did I just say thread again?), holding various conversation, not all about quilts. At one table three or four helped with a design, at another table all sewed the same block. I listened for a moment and thought how happy I felt. Yes, that room, in spite of what may be personal circumstances, was filled with happiness. I thought, "These people are really a nice bunch of people!" I also knew no matter what life brings, they are there for me!

Looking back, I am so grateful because today I know what I would have missed had I not gone that first Tuesday morning, and I can't imagine my life minus that!

You Need to Do What You Love

by **KRISTIN GREER-BENTON**
Mexico, New York

I started quilting a year and a half ago when I found out my father had cancer. I was always a crafter without a favorite medium, and I wanted to do something for him. I decided a quilt would be best so that when he went to his chemo he would know that we (my family) were with him.

It was a quick and easy pattern but special all the same. He really liked it and told me how talented I was. He wanted me to do something with my talent. He was young and so was I. (He was 61 and I was 36). I found a love for fabric and a heartfelt desire to keep quilting.

Unfortunately, my father passed away two months later. It was very quick and we struggled a lot. We were a very close family and there was a huge hole in our lives. My parents best friends were there for us every step of the way and were so supportive I felt I needed to do something for them. I found a fabric that very much reminded me of my parents

and them. So I stitched, and I cried, and sometimes I needed to quit because I couldn't see through the tears, but I made them a quilt.

It was beautiful, meaningful, filled with memories, and we laughed, cried, and hugged. I needed to create more; I couldn't stop. So I made eight quilted sleeping bags for Christmas that year. When Christmas was done I looked around for more reasons to quilt. My father's brother and my mother's brother needed love. They both live alone in California. Neither of them was ever married and neither of them ever had kids. My mother and her brother lost two sisters and my father in three years time. My father and his brother lost their mother five years ago to cancer and now my uncle was the only one left on his side of the family. So what did I do? I made quilts and drove them to California.

I realized in the last two years of my life that time goes by way too fast and you need to do what you love. So I dove head-first into quilting and haven't stopped yet. I love every minute of it and now I have two nieces on the way to make our lives fuller and my stash a little lighter. I can't wait.

I hope to someday open a quilt shop of my own. I now have a passion that I want to carry on for decades and my daughter, who is six, wants to learn how to sew with me. It gets a little crowded with her in my chair but I don't mind. Someday she won't be able to fit anymore, so I will squeeze her in as long as she will let me.

I have fit 20 quilts into my first year and a half of quilting. They are not perfect but they are made with all the love I can sew into them, and I can't wait to make more.

The Passing Quilt

by **DEBBIE LANCASTER**
Seaside, Oregon

In 2005, my friend Bobbie, who lives across the street from me, got a visit from her brother. An older man 20 years my senior. A nice man, Billy from Oklahoma, soft spoken, sweet, and sick.

I became friends over the months with him. One morning Bobbie called to tell me Billy had decided he wanted a wife... and it was me. I laughed; I had decided long ago never to marry again. The joke was on me though, because after six months of pestering, I fell for this crazy, lovable guy and we were married.

As I said, he was sick and we had four years together before he died. His last stay in the hospital is why this story ends with quilting. With our family all around his hospital bed a nun came into the room with a beautiful quilt and lay it over him. She told us it was called a Passing Quilt, and that it had been made by quilters in my town. I was to take

Photo Courtesy Debbie Lancaster

it home with me after he passed and they hoped it would bring me comfort. Well it did and still does.

I wanted to be a part of this group so I called the hospital to get the information and met these ladies. I bought a little sewing machine from Costco and started learning how to quilt online. Leah Day, Craftsy, the Fons gals, and of course Jenny Doan all taught me to quilt. That was over four years ago and I now have a Bernina, a sewing room, and a couple hundred quilts under my belt. And I quilt for the Passing Quilt Program which meets once a month to make quilts for the comfort of others. My Billy would be pleased.

The Flower Garden

by **ASHLEY COPELAND**
Springfield, Missouri

I was born into a family of quilters. I have spent many years watching my mother, grandmother, and aunts piece beautiful quilts. As I've grown up, I have seen my mother make a bounty of wonderful quilts that she has given away. Naturally, I followed suit. I am going to tell the story of the only quilt I've kept for myself.

Last January, my husband and I found out we were pregnant. We were both excited and nervous about becoming parents. In May, we went to the doctor ecstatic to find out the gender and start the real planning.

We saw we were having a boy, but the excitement only lasted a few minutes before the doctor came in and told us about several concerns she had with the ultrasound. After some genetic testing a few weeks later, we found out there was a 99 percent probability our little boy had a genetic abnormality that generally results in stillbirth. The doctor told us there was nothing she could do and we shouldn't expect any more

Photo Courtesy Ashley Copeland

than two weeks with him if he made it to birth. If he made it, the hospital didn't have the resources to help him.

Trusting in God's ability to work through both miracles and medicine, we decided to go to different doctors in another city who were willing to help us have more time with him once he was born, even if just a few months or years.

God's plan for Nolan wasn't a miracle or medicine, at least not in the conventional sense. We lost him in August at 33 weeks.

Throughout our entire journey, God gave me an overwhelming sense of peace in His plan. One of the best illustrations of this is a flower garden. When I pick flowers out of my garden, it doesn't make them any less beautiful or less valuable, it just means I want them inside to adorn my table. I had the same sense of what God had done with our son. His life was full and complete, but God wanted him for heaven.

A few days after leaving the hospital, I started Nolan's quilt. I used raw edge appliqué to paint a bright and comforting picture of God pulling Nolan out of his flower garden. Every day, I have moments of hurt and brokenness, but the quilt is a reminder that God didn't take Nolan from me — He chose Nolan for heaven.

The 'Stolen' Quilt

by **CAROL INMAN**
Concordia, Missouri

I am the first of five daughters-in-law for my mother-in-law. The family was helping pack their things for the move from the farm to town. I opened a dresser drawer and there were 20 large Dresden Plate circles, all stitched with 1930s fabric, many feed sacks. When questioned, my mother-in-law told me she pieced them when she was expecting my hubby, her firstborn, who was 63 by then. She proceeded to point out many of the prints and tell me where she or her sister wore that dress, or her brother wore that shirt, etc. I was amazed! I asked her what she planned to do with them and she felt she might get them appliquéd to some muslin and quilt it at some point.

So the first time the family was together in their new home, I sneaked one circle out, appliquéd it to a base fabric and showed it to her. She then told me I didn't have to "steal" the rest, I could just have them. I purchased some retro 1930s fabric at the "It's A Gatherin'" show in

Stover, Missouri that year, and finished the quilt. My mother-in-law was speechless when she saw it and said it was exactly what she envisioned she would do "someday." I entered it in our local fall festival where I received a second place ribbon, but the story I printed with it created lots of interest. My daughter will receive the quilt when I no longer want it. Right now, it is on our bed where I can see it and remember what a treasure I "stole" from my mother-in-law.

The Ninety Year Quilt

by **PAT PALMERIO**
Downington, Pennsylvania

Quilting was never something I thought about until one day when I was cleaning out my closet. I rediscovered a very old brown paper bag that I had carefully stored several years before. In the bag, there was a small stack of fabric squares which had been pieced together by my grandmother and had been passed on to me by my mother. I had no idea what to do with the squares when they were originally given to me.

My grandmother died in 1927 when my mother was only two years old. Because she was so young at the time, my mother has no recollection of her own mom. This small stack of fabric squares was a fragile and special connection to the past. Each square was made from shirt fabric, most probably old shirts that my grandfather had worn. And in the bag was a piece of the brown paper bag on which my grandmother had written her initials.

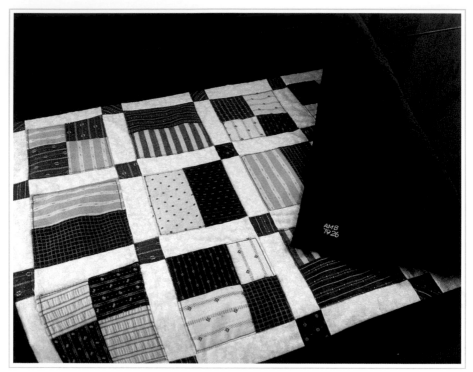

Right about the time of rediscovering the squares, I saw a Missouri Star Quilt Co. tutorial. It was then that I decided that I would use whatever squares I could salvage to finish what my grandmother had started so long ago. Carefully cutting and piecing the squares, I made a small quilt and gave it to my mother as a surprise. A gift from her mother and her daughter, almost 90 years in the making!

I embroidered my grandmothers initials on the back with the date she started it - 1926. To be sure, the quilt isn't perfect, but in our family, it is a treasure!

A Childhood Love

✳

by **KARIN SCHMIDT**
Victoria, Australia

To tell you my quilt story, I have to take you back to the year 1945. After living through a horrid time in East Germany, my mother took my brother and me on a very difficult trip to West Germany. On the arrival there I was so ill that I was sent to a rescue children's home on the Island Foehr in North Friesland.

Here the children received food, clothing, and best of all, each child had his or her own bed. Each bed was covered with a quilt made by women in America. More about the quilts, I do not know. Can anyone today believe what that meant to us children? Each quilt was different, so we all had our own, which gave us a feeling of happiness. This is the time I fell in love with quilting.

Many years have passed and I have lived in Australia for more than 50 years. I never forgot the beauty of this first quilt, but I never thought I would be able to create something so wonderful and never tried it.

The children's home Marienhof as it was in 1946. These children all had a their own bed covered with a quilt made by women from America.

Two years ago I moved to a retirement village and there I found a very active patchwork group. People there encouraged me to have a go. Now at an age of 77, I have started and find a day without sewing wasted time. Your tutorials, dear Jenny, have made it so easy for me and I thank you. However, I am writing this letter most of all to thank your American ladies, whoever they are, for thinking of the lost children of the Second World War and bringing some joy to us in a very difficult time.

Last year our group made quilts for a new aged home and I was able to contribute two myself. No guess what it reminded me of.

Pass It On

by **FRANCES TEMPELMEIER**
O'Fallon, Missouri

began quilting in 2001. I had been thinking about learning this art form for many years because of a gift my husband and I received on our wedding day. My husband's parents both died of cancer before I had a chance to meet them. When my mother-in-law learned that she was terminal, she got busy and made some quilts for my husband. Two were to be given to him on his wedding day and two more when he had his first child. There was also a handwritten note with the quilts.

These quilts had a huge impact on me and I wondered if I could learn to make something this beautiful. Over the years these quilts were used and loved. One went with me each time I went to the hospital to have a baby.

When my children were in high school I decided it was time to pass on this tradition; I wanted to learn as much as possible about quilting. I began taking classes, reading blogs, and buying quilting books. My skills evolved and I wanted to share this art form with my students. (I taught for 37 years.) So each year we made a quilt to be donated to the school auction to raise money. The students always signed these quilts.

I have made quilts for my children and now I am quilting for my grandchildren. My granddaughter has four quilts and my soon-to-be-born grandchild also has four quilts. Of course, I have many quilts in my home which will eventually be passed on to my children. I think my mother-in-law would be proud of all the quilts I have made.

Full to the Brim

by **KATHY HAYDYSCH**
Louisburg, North Carolina

uilting was just one of those things I always wanted to learn, but did not really know anything about. My grandmother, Nana, always sewed and taught me so much about so many things, but did not quilt. I still hear her telling me, "The back of your work should look as neat as the front."

Our kids grew up. I was working full time and life was going along until July of 2009, when I was diagnosed with breast cancer. I thought to myself, "WHAT? There is still so much I want to do." But life can kick you in the teeth just so you can see what you're made of. With the love and support of my family and wonderful doctors I started this journey through treatment and surgery. In 2010 I was cancer-free and decided that it was time to empty that bucket instead of carrying it around full of things I wanted to do someday.

Our annual quilting retreat in North Carolina.

I looked online and found a quilt shop not far from home that gave classes. I called for information regarding a beginner class. I was told it was starting that night and invited to come by. Of course I said, "I can't come tonight." I didn't have fabric or my sewing machine and there would be no time to go home and get it and make it back for the class. Again, here is that sisterhood so commonly experienced with this art. The shop owner, Betsy, said "Come on in, we will help get your fabric picked out and there is a shop machine you can use for tonight." So I called my husband and said, "I won't be home for dinner. I'm going to learn how to quilt." His response was "Well, ok then. Have fun."

And fun I had! It was a small class. We started with a sampler that was filled with great techniques and patterns, but was not too overwhelming. I was a little nervous but knew I was in the right place when I met our teacher, Jean, as well as Liz and Nancy, who were taking the class. Jean was good at giving us instruction along with tips, and she made it fun.

Over a period of six classes we finished our sampler. But in those six weeks so much more than learning to quilt happened. I formed some of the dearest relationships of my life and to this day don't know where I would be without these ladies from the beginner class I took three years ago. We celebrate highs, huddle up for the lows, and are a constant support system for each other. We are still quilting together. We attend an annual retreat where we make a project for charity among other projects where we continue to learn from each other. And we laugh. You have never heard so much laughing. It was suggested that Depends should be a must-have when packing for the retreat!

They say when you give a quilt away, you give your heart. But what they didn't tell me was when you learn to quilt, your heart fills to the brim.

Ode to Quilting

by **JUDITH WILLIAMS**
Eagan, Minnesota

A milestone birthday is approaching. If I had a mind to, I could wallpaper the bathroom with ads for Medicare supplements. How did this happen? One day I was a young mom making clothes for my little girls, and then I was a great grammie, ready for Medicare. Yikes!

Time for learning something new. But what will it be? Okay, it will be crafty. I am, after all, a crafty gal. When my youngest daughter moved out, I inherited my art grotto (a room for crafting in my basement). Paper. Yarn. Fabric. I love them all. What to master next?

My cousin quilts. Beautifully. Dare I try?
I check Pinterest. I check YouTube. I check my stash of sewing supplies. I make a list. I check it twice. I find out quilt stores are pretty nice. But I digress. My first project is done. A table runner. It looks good. I covered the wonky places with rickrack.

And I am ready for project number two. I am a quilter.

Good Advice

by **MARY LATHAM**
Cory, Indiana

While laying in bed with our six year old grandson, he looked at me and said, "Booie, I don't want you to get old." I figured what he was thinking, but asked anyway. He said, "When you get old you will die."

I said, "Keith why don't I make you something to remember me by?" I got out some pictures of quilts. He then looked at me and said, "Booie, you better hurry!" I was only 66 at the time.

I have since made him two quilts, plus three more for the other three grandchildren. I call them penny angel quilts. Each one has a small lace angel on it and a penny wrapped in plastic under the angels head. The penny is minted the year of their birth. The kids were my inspiration. Please believe me, I am not good at matching squares or points, I just have fun in doing it and I enjoy leaving some part of me for them.

I have never laughed so hard as I did when this little guy said I needed to hurry. It was a treasured moment.

Unfinished

by **SUSAN BUTLER**
Houston, Texas

In 1956 at the age of four, I sat by my mother's side as she sewed on her Singer 15-91. The sound of the scissors, her deft hands, the glow from the light of the machine are memories that fill my mind and heart with total comfort. She taught me how to sew by hand when I was five. She let me actually sew on her machine a year later. Once she was certain I could master the machinery, she gave me wings. My only rule to follow was to not leave a mess!

My mother died suddenly of a heart attack when I was 30 years old and the darkest cloud in my life took over. We were connected in many ways with our crafting, sewing, cooking and gardening, and my love for her was profound as for my father, as well. We had enjoyed the new craze for quilting in the early '70s and it was my thrill to take personal hand quilting lessons here in Houston from Jewel Patterson, mother of the founder of the International Quilt Festival. I still pull out the box of

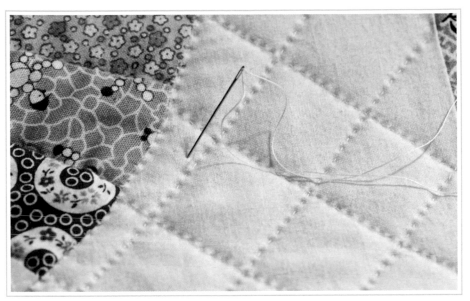

Photo Courtesy Susan Butler

things my mother and I were last working on in 1983 when she died, and just look and feel the pieces of fabric. I think about changes in the industry and how she would be amazed at the new gadgets! A rotary cutter, oh my!

I have been a bond broker for 31 years, something I am very grateful for. My work is good. It makes those hours of the day when I get to play after work all that much sweeter. Place me in the corner for the most unfinished projects, it does not matter to me. When I am at my favorite sewing machine, my mother's Singer 15-91, I feel that peace and comfort from the sound of the machine to the sound of the scissors. Sometimes when I mess up I'll say a bad word and that makes me laugh and remember my mother's times like that too!

Life is filled with a variety of compartments for feelings. Fabric makes me feel appreciation to the artist that designed the image, the company that manufactured the fabric, and the merchant that puts up with a lot to offer the fabric for sale. I have too much fabric. Each piece in my possession is used to look at, feel, and think. It gives me that feeling of contentment. Passionately calm moments await me in my sewing room.

I don't aspire to be a great artist and create works for grandness. I tremendously admire those that do and they inspire me and keep my mind racing with ideas. I enjoy simply grabbing those satisfying feelings of comfort that cannot be matched in any other way. I plan on buying too much fabric.

The Visit

by **SUE WAGNER**
Bella Vista, Arizona

A friend opened my eyes and heart to quilting almost three years ago, and if you ask my hubs and daughter, I've become obsessed! My goal was to complete a quilting project every month or two, and since I retired this year, my goal is to create a new project weekly. Most of the quilts I create are lovingly given to family and friends, with many donated to Quilts of Valor, Arkansas Children's Hospital, underprivileged children, women's shelter, and others. However, of the quilts made so far, my favorite story is as follows.

When helping at a quilting booth at War Eagle, Arizona in 2012, a gal came to ask if I could make a quilt out of her dad's old shirts, some stained, some with holes, etc. He had passed the previous year, and she wanted to surprise her mom with an everyday reminder of him, a meaningful gift she wanted to give her mom for Christmas. She stated she felt her dad had "visited" her and her sister over the past year through dreams and/or strong feelings, but her mom was disheartened as he had never "visited" her.

The week before the gal gave her mom the quilt, made out of a dozen or so shirts, her mom called to say her dad finally "visited" the previous night. He was standing at the foot of her bed, and although she couldn't see his legs or head clearly, his shirts kept changing as he watched her — the same shirts that were assembled into this quilt! What a shock it was when the woman's daughter presented her with this quilt! Her mom cherishes it, taking it everywhere she goes, even on short jaunts to the grocery store (although she leaves it in the car!). The daughter has since had me make her a similar quilt with the leftovers of her mom's quilt.

This inspired me to quilt even more! I joined the local quilting guild, bought online classes, attended quilt shows, made friends with many of the local shops and quilters. I regularly quilt with friends, and LOVE Jenny's tutorials. MSQC makes my quilts look more advanced than just a beginner, too, which motivates me to quilt even more! But enough of reading this, it's time to get quilting!

Great-Grandma Emma's Quilt

by **BARBARA BREAZEALE BICKFORD**
Rocklin, California

I grew up surrounded by women. My mother had seven sisters, my father had two. I had ten girl cousins that lived close and were within five years of my age. I am also one of four girls and my two sisters each had four daughters. I'm the only one who sews. Of my nine aunts, only one sewed and she specialized in wedding dresses.

My parents had a very limited income and I realized early that if I wanted clothes I would have to make them, so I started sewing my own clothes when I was in the seventh grade. I have a picture of myself in that first dress I made. It had a seam right down the front. Why didn't anyone tell me plaids are supposed to match?

It wasn't until the late 1970s when I had three small boys that I became interested in quilting. I bought cute animal panels, cut out the animals, and sewed them to a piece of gingham. Then I tied it together with

a thick polyester bat and a plain-colored back. I showed them to my Mom and she said, "Maybe you'd be interested in that quilt your great-grandma gave me in 1948."

My mom explained that Great-Grandma Emma gave it to her when she was newly married and thought she needed something to do. It was the makings of a quilt really. And yes, I was interested.

As I looked at the pieces in the box my mom gave me, a strange sensation came over me. My Great-Grandma Emma had died before I was born but here were pieces of fabric she had picked out, cut, and sewed. That sealed my future. From that day forward I was a quilter. Not a good quilter...a quilter.

I joined the older ladies at my church that quilted each week, and Nettie, Bessie, Velma, and Violet were my fellow quilters and mentors. I took my first quilting class in the 1990s. Then I took a big step and joined the Pioneer Quilters Guild in 2004. I wasn't sure what a guild did. I expected to learn about quilting. I expected to make a few friends. But I received a pleasant surprise. I found a vibrant group of women that work to not only make their own quilts, but spread their talents to the less fortunate. I found that a passion for quilting is the common thread that binds our members together.

Long Arm or Husband's Arm?

by **TED AND CHRIS ZEIGLER**
Wellsville, Pennsylvania

I started quilting when our children were very young, about 35 years ago. Like most families, life got busy and I didn't have much time to quilt. I started to quilt again about 15 or 20 years ago, getting back to what I really love to do. I took some classes and loved to see what others do at quilt shows.

My husband decided he wanted to try hand quilting after he had knee surgery and needed something to do. He found he really liked it and he's a pretty good quilter too. Now when there's a quilt in the frame, that's where you'll find him. Three years ago he was diagnosed with a muscular disease and has trouble walking. He used to do blacksmithing but is not able to do it because he has lost his strength to swing a hammer. Quilting has been a blessing because it gives him something wonderful to do. While other quilters may piece a quilt together and take them to a shop to be quilted by a longarm, I take mine to the kitchen to be quilted by my husband's arm.

We got our first computer about a year ago and if I didn't do anything else on it I would want it to follow MSQC. My very first purchase on the computer was the Front Porch bundle. The morning it appeared as the Daily Deal, my husband was still in bed. When he got up I told him he was my first love, but I had fallen in love again. He looked at me with a puzzled expression. When I showed him the fabric, the nice man he is, he said, "Well go ahead and order it." I did and we love it. My second purchase was *Block* Magazine, which I ordered before he was even out of bed. When I told him about *Block*, he said, "What are you waiting for? Order it." I was happy to tell him I already did. We both love it even though I drove him nuts waiting for the mail lady.

Helping Me Finish My Quilt

by **DENISE CAFFEY**
Kansas City, Missouri

My love of quilting began with my mentor, my mother. My mom was a wonderful seamstress and later in life decided to take up quilting. She taught me the basics and I learned to love it. I started with small projects and worked my way into the more difficult ones.

In March of 2004, I decided to take on a rather large project, a queen size quilt named "Shimmer" by Joy Hoffman. With pattern in hand, I headed to the local quilt store and the cutting began.

In April of the same year, my mom was diagnosed with ovarian cancer. I am an ultrasound technologist by profession, so I knew she had a big challenge ahead. My quilting project was put on hold with a more important battle to help with. My mom faced her challenge with all she had. After two years and two months, on June 5, 2006, she lost her fight to this silent killer. The wife of 50 years, mother of five, grandmother of nine, and great-grandmother of one was taken from us.

The following year was a difficult one for us all.

After several attempts, I finally decided it was time to finish my challenge. I pulled out the project and after many days of sewing, with memories of my mom (and a few tears), I finished my quilt. It was time to take the quilt to my quilter.

When I purchased my fabrics, I did not buy backing fabric, so back to the quilt store I went. With over three years passed, I inquired about the fabrics I had purchased. "We no longer carry that group of fabrics," I was told. Through the bolts of fabrics, I began my search, hoping to find something I could use. I made my way to the reduced corner of the store to check one last place. There on the top shelf was a bolt of fabric from the line of fabrics I had used. I don't know who was more surprised that they still had any in the store, me or the woman helping me cut the fabric. I needed seven yards and there were seven and a half on the bolt.

As I left the store with my fabric, I knew my mom was with me that day. I had been with her throughout her challenge and now she was helping me to finish mine.

Every time I see this quilt I think of my mom. We all have our challenges to face throughout our lives. While quilting, remember someone or something in your life that has helped you through yours.

Thanks mom, I miss you and love you.
-Denise

A Match Made in Quilting Heaven

by **JANE AND JOHN WELCH**
Murray, Kentucky

Hello, we are Jane and John Welch and our story began 47 years ago on a blind date! We married at a very early age and have done almost everything together (you know, through sickness and health) and now that we have found MSQC, there is no chance for wealth!

My mother was a purist and pieced and quilted completely by hand and I was not interested. However, when she died in 2002, I began to realize that there was something about quilting that I wanted to investigate. So I took a class and was hopelessly hooked.

John has always supported my sewing and even bought me a wonderful Singer sewing machine for Mother's Day the first year we were married. Although he would willingly accompany me to fabric stores, he never showed any interest in actually participating. Imagine my surprise when, at age 62, he said he would like to make a quilt!

Photo Courtesy Jane and John Welch

He chose a log cabin lap-size for his first project and it took him three hours to pick out his fabric. He learned a lot and did a beautiful job. We sew together in a converted bedroom. We each have our own machines and other supplies but we share the cutting table and a large ironing table. John prefers pastels and light colors and I normally go with the dark!

Over the past four years, we have made quilt samples for a local fabric store, gifted each of our children and grandchildren with a special quilt for Christmas, made dozens of charity quilts, and made quilts for no reason at all. We maintain a balanced life by having outside activities alone with friends but happily spend hours sewing together listening to music. We have so much fun each day and never ever have to say, "There is nothing to do!" We hope that we are able to continue doing what we love together for a long, long time.

Just a Wad of Fabric

by **LEE MARX**
San Miguel, California

A couple of years ago, my mother was ill and dying. It seemed everywhere I went shopping there were these little wads of fabric tied in raffia or cloth strips in little baskets on display. The colors and feel of the fabrics were pleasing. I was into flowers at the time, roses to be specific. So for a few dollars, I would buy a wad or two of fabric to share with Mom.

My father had this amazing rose garden at his and Mom's cottage at the lake. Every day he would bring in fresh-cut flowers to set by her bedside or on the little table by her chair when she had the energy to be up. We had a dozen vases of fresh flowers in the house at any given time. Everyone enjoyed putting the freshest flowers out for Mom.

By the time Mom passed away, I had a dozen or so wads of fabric that I would unroll, look at, feel, and remember - lovely dark green prints, pale pink bouquet prints, and some with lavish roses splashed across them.

A few months after Mom's memorial service, Dad wanted to visit his sisters, who live just a couple hours drive away. I took my wads of fabric with me thinking maybe I could make something out of them, as my Aunties are master quilters. Oh how the Aunties laughed at my description of these "wads of fabric!" They immediately set to work on my vocabulary, plying me with "recipes," handout sheets, and a YouTube video of very funny woman with a great laugh, some kind of pizza roller, a cutting board that healed itself, and an iron that stood up on legs after she had pressed her seams to the dark side! We had only come for the day, but we stayed a couple of nights. A quilter was being born.

I have been piecing for a little over a year now. I was shopping last weekend and sure enough, in the back in baskets on display were some "wads of fabric." For a few dollars, I purchased enough fat quarters of roses to make another memory.

If You Want Something Done Right, Learn to Quilt!

by **KATIE PAUGH**
Washington Court House, Ohio

My husband and I were married for seven years with no luck of conceiving a child. Finally, we stopped trying so hard, we relaxed, and we gave our worries to God. Sure enough, He blessed us with a beautiful baby girl.

I'm a fairly typical (crazy!) first time mom. I take TONS of pictures, I document milestones, I keep all of her clothes and favorite outfits. Then I decided that I didn't want to box up all those cute clothes and never look at them again. I decided I needed to get a quilt made from all of her clothes that were our favorites.

I searched and searched for someone who knew how to make a t-shirt quilt, seeing how I didn't even own a sewing machine, let alone know how to work one. I finally found a girl who lived near us and she was reasonably priced. I dropped off my daughter's clothes to her and

about two months later she sent me an email telling me she wasn't comfortable doing it and she sent the clothes back.

That's when I decided I was going to teach myself to sew and make my daughter's t-shirt quilt on my own. My mom bought me a sewing machine for Christmas, and with the help of the Internet (especially Jenny Doan's tutorials!), I taught myself how to sew.

It took me several months, but I made it! I included all of my daughter's "My First..." shirts (my first Christmas, my first Easter, etc.), the shirt she wore on her first trip to the zoo, shirts given as gifts from special people, etc. Every t-shirt has a story. We have snuggled under that quilt every night since.

Since then, I have made my daughter a heavier quilt to keep her warm on cold nights and a quilt to comfort her at nap time while she's at the babysitter's. I see how much she is comforted by them (and how comforting it is to snuggle under our t-shirt quilt after a long day), and now we make quilts for charities so that other kids can be comforted too.

My grandmother passed away several years ago and I asked my mom if I could have her wooden wind chimes. For some reason I was drawn to them. Just recently I found out that those wooden chimes are actually made out of old industrial-size wooden spools! I couldn't believe it. God knows things about us WAY before we do!

Thanks, Mom

by **SUZANN HURFORD**
Belleville, Wisconsin

During the summer of 2012, I was planning a trip back to my home state of New Mexico to visit my mother. One of the phone conversations we had about my upcoming trip involved her asking me if I would be interested in finishing a Christmas appliqué quilt that she had started several years earlier.

Keep in mind that my previous sewing experiences were extremely limited. My mother, bless her heart, had attempted many times to teach me to sew on her sewing machine but all such attempts had usually ended with me in tears, the sewing machine bobbin tangled into knots, and the sewing project ruined. I had convinced myself that I was domestically challenged when it came to the world of sewing. However, I had always loved quilts and had for years harbored a secret dream of someday making my own. When Mom's offer came, I decided to take her up on it, with the stipulation being that she would have to walk me through it step-by-step since I hadn't a clue how to quilt or even where to begin.

I was to fly out on Tuesday, July 3rd and spend the next week with her. I eagerly counted down the days, looking forward to not only the time I would get to spend with my mother, but the quilting lessons I was going to receive as well. However, two days before my flight I received a call from my brother saying that Mom had suffered a major heart attack and wasn't expected to make it.

My plans immediately changed. I rushed to my mother's side where she had fallen into a coma and I remained with her until she passed away just a few days later. In the days and months to follow, as my brother and I began to sort through her things, we ran across the pieces of the Christmas quilt she had started. I brought them home with me, along with her old sewing machine, vowing that someday, somehow I was going to finish that quilt.

It took me a few months to gather up my nerve, but I eventually bought a few self-teaching quilting books, and slowly began to teach myself the basics of quilting. I wasn't quite ready to dive into the world of appliqué just yet, but figured if I could learn the quilting basics, eventually I could work myself up to it. I remember sitting down with Mom's old Singer 301 that first day and saying to it, "Okay, pal. It's just you and me now. We've got to find a way to get along. She's not here anymore."

And miraculously, that old sewing machine and I did make peace. For the next few months, I learned all about rotary cutting, quarter-inch seams, and the importance of pressing seams correctly. The more I learned the more excited I got, and before I knew it a passion had been ignited. What started out as a simple desire to honor my mother has turned into a life-long love of quilting. I haven't finished Mom's Christmas quilt yet. I've only just begun to teach myself how to appliqué. But I will get there and someday I'll have that quilt completed and be able to pass it down to my daughter.

Why do I quilt? I quilt to feel close to my mother. I quilt to honor her memory. I quilt because it brings me joy to make something so beautiful. I love quilts. I love wrapping myself up in them. For me, it's like getting a warm, loving hug. And to know that I can now make something so special and send these special 'hugs' out to other people is a wonderful gift. Thanks, Mom.

When Your Husband Knows Best

by **ARLENE OSBORN**
Albany, Australia

I really didn't have time to do any sewing as I cared for my son who was totally dependant and had profound disabilities. When he died at age 26, I was absolutely lost. I would wander around the house not knowing what to do with myself.

Then my husband took me into our local fabric store and told me to buy a cutting mat, ruler, and cutter as I was going to learn how to quilt. I straight away said NO WAY but he insisted. Even the owner was a bit hesitant but my husband insisted, so out I came with my three items wondering what I was going to do with them.

He got a friend of mine to take me to her sewing club which was held once a month. I went there not knowing what I was doing, but I began to get inspired. Still not knowing what to do, as the sewing club was not a quilting club, it was mainly for embroidery and dressmaking.

I came home a bit disappointed but I thought that as I had spent the money purchasing the three items I was going to have to use them. So back I went to the fabric shop and spoke to the lady who worked there and took a book of blocks I had bought. I picked a block and told her that I wanted to do that particular block, a bowtie pattern. She sold me the fabric I needed and sent me on my way.

I was too scared to cut the fabric as I had no idea what I was doing. So back I went to the shop and the clerk, Jenny, showed me how to cut the fabric. Then I found out that apart from the sewing club the shop ran a quilting class, so I was in.

I had cared for my son for 26 years and I thought that quilting had to be easier than that. Now I spend nearly every day quilting. I love it, I am definitely hooked and I am sure that I am going to die with the most fabric.

I wish my son was still alive as I would have made him a few quilts, but I have grandchildren whom I sew for and I am always making new quilts to give to someone.

I have made many friends through quilting and as I suffer with severe depression, this is a wonderful way to spend my time. So now when I buy more fabric and my husband gives me one of his leering looks, I cheekily remind him about just who started me off on this adventure.